SAVE *the* LAST DANCE

SAVE *the* LAST DANCE

POEMS

Gerald Stern

W. W. NORTON & COMPANY

New York • London

For information about permission to reproduce selections from this book,
write to Permissions, W. W. Norton & Company, Inc.,
500 Fifth Avenue, New York, NY 10110

For information about special discounts for bulk purchases, please contact
W. W. Norton Special Sales at specialsales@wwnorton.com or 800-233-4830

Manufacturing by Courier Westford
Book design by Chris Welch
Production manager: Julia Druskin

Library of Congress Cataloging-in-Publication Data

Stern, Gerald, date.
Save the last dance : poems / Gerald Stern. — 1st ed.
p. cm.
ISBN 978-0-393-06612-8
I. Title.
PS3569.T3888S28 2008
811'.54—dc22

                                        2007052327

W. W. Norton & Company, Inc.
500 Fifth Avenue, New York, N.Y. 10110
www.wwnorton.com

W. W. Norton & Company Ltd.
Castle House, 75/76 Wells Street, London W1T 3QT

1 2 3 4 5 6 7 8 9 0

In loving memory of Grace Paley

(1922–2007)

CONTENTS

Part I

Part II

Part III

SAVE *the* LAST DANCE

Part I

DIOGENES

Diogenes for me and sleeping in a bathtub
and stealing the key to the genealogy room
close to the fake Praxiteles and ripping
a book up since the wrath had taken me
over the edge again and you understand
as no one else how when the light is lit
I have to do something, I couldn't hold my arm up
for nothing, I couldn't stand on the top step
barking—I'll put it this way, living in a room
two cellars down was good, I got to smell
the earth, I carried a long red wire down
with a bulb attached—after that it never mattered.

Traveling backwards in time is almost nothing
for here is the brain and with it I have relived
one thing after another but I am wavering
at *only* reliving though what is hard is being there—
I don't know what the Germans called it, existing,
non-existing, both at once, there is a
rose explaining it, or it's a table;
imagine that, from one tree and its branches
once it was rooted, once the leaves were glabrous
and coruscating, then came everything.

THOM McCANN

This was to be free of the burden of representation,
to put your feet in an X-ray machine and thereby
not only get cancer and not only get fitted up
with the perfect pair of shoes, but thence to grieve
how thin your bones looked, how like more like a bird
you were than an ape and how you mourned how huge
your feet were and you went to the machine oh every
ten minutes or so and how that leather pinched
for it was more cardboard than cow and how it was
inevitable the limping, it was called
the breaking in, I wanted to tell you this.

1 9 5 0

I was the one who lived in that room and it was
Liz we lured there though we tossed a coin first
and I was in a dead sleep when the two of them
arrived in the morning one of them disheveled
and one of them pert who after he left we lay
like cardboard in the narrow bed I bought
the stockings for and took her home on the subway
or where she worked maybe and after my classes
I climbed six floors again to sit and stare
from my small desk in front of the portholes and wander
off from time to time to the sink in the hall
nor was there a rug or a lamp and it was the year
they turned the lights on and my Bible was stolen.

I get the sense that she is not cooperative in English
and on the last leg of her trip into New York City
going through the tunnel and briefly through the light
and into another tunnel but this time for good
she sits until the line is in front of her,
singing a little Christmas chanty, her nose
running but otherwise decent, the smile extreme
but not forced, the coffee stains nothing, the ugly
lying tabloid under her feet, whatever the
language is, also nothing, and I, eternal
sucker, I rub my eyes for I belong to
a certain breed of men who when the train jerks
then slows down on the platform it is a drama
extreme, and there was a time I wouldn't have lost her,
and also a time I followed someone, I say it
with shame and mortification, for half a day
because I couldn't bear it, I would have lost
everything, I hung on to a thread. How
was it different with Dante? Though I ended
lost—and entangled—however he ended.

WHAT FOR?

1946 there was an overcoat
with rows of buttons fifteen dollars and two
American flags for some ungodly reason
and a slight rise in the distance as the street
went over the river for which I would have breathed
the air both in and out since I was a bellows
and one by one my lungs were ruined but I wouldn't
change my life, what for? You wouldn't know
unless you crossed the river yourself, unless you
climbed a hill and turned around twice
to stare at the street behind you, either mud
or cobblestone, and count the wooden steps
or look through the windows longingly, the houses
piled up the one below the next, the dirt
supreme, your breathing heavy, the base of a cliff
even further below, a river shining from
time to time, your mind half-empty, your teacher
a curbstone, the mountain really hill upon hill;
you know the details, the porches pulled you up,
your face turned white at a certain point, I'm sure
you walked through a cloud how slow you learned, how
        absurd
the goats of Arcady or the baskets of apples
in New Jerusalem compared to that.

From where I sit, given the time of year,
the light comes only between the trees, but there is
water, and at four in the evening, given our
latitude and the direction we face, the sun
lights up what seems, from where I sit, more like
a pool and I am changed for a minute, though it
is a river, you can depend on that, I crossed
from time to time and lived on for a while
and was assured that way the hundreds of nights
I walked my mile and ended up at the hot
waterfall and the gears of the nineteenth century
above the high brick wall I rested under.

The whole point was getting rid of glut
for which I starved myself and lived with the heat down
and only shaved oh every five days and used
a blunt razor for months so that my cheek
was not only red but the hair was bent not cut
for which I then would be ready for the bicycle
and the broken wrist, for which—oh God—I would be
ready to climb the steps and fight the boxes
with only nothing, a pair of shoes, and once
inside to open the window and let the snow in
and when the fire was over climb down the icy
fire escape and drop the last twenty
feet with notebooks against my chest, bruises
down one side of my body, fresh blood down the other.

BRONZE ROOSTERS

How love of every single human creature
took place in my life and how it lasted for almost
a week but I had a fever; and the day
I realized finally I had to give up
running for I had lost the will, almost the
muscles themselves, I was confused since I
was never a runner as an adult, and on the
last day I was taking my antibiotics
I lost a small pink pill while in between
reading the labels, or I convinced myself
that that was the case and it took me almost an hour
to stop my coughing I was in such a state,
and I was light-headed walking over the bricks
and had to hold on to my wooden fence, amazed
that we could last the way we do compared to
birds just blown by the wind, their locomotion
beyond themselves, or ants and beetles, God,
what does the mind do there, or bronze roosters?

She was a darling with her roses, though what I
like is lavender for I can dry it and
nothing is blue like that, so here I am,
in my arms a bouquet of tragic lavender,
the whole history of Southern France against my
chest, the fields stretching out, the armies
killing each other, horses falling, Frenchmen
dying by the thousands, though none for love.

As if some creature down there was having a smoke
and there was a lamp with fringes and a rug
so filthy the earth was red and the blue flowers
were black and there was nothing to read and only
a shovel in my face, for such it is
under the lid that I rocked forever and changed
my clay pipe every hour; and reading what
was left of the Psalms, for they were torn and eaten,
I did so by holding a candle over my head;
and I was careful of water for in Them it says
God is filled with water and in Them it says
the valleys shout with joy, which I do here;
and also I whistle in spite of the dirt in my mouth,
and I still hate oppression and I hate slander
where there was a brick outhouse and a library
down from the kitchen and the butchered backyard maple.

Not infrequently destroyed as bits of paper
of no value by the women in my family,
namely Ida, Libby, and the maid Thelma,
my drawings were gone by the time I was eleven
and so I turned to music and led orchestras
walking through the woods; and Saturday nights
we feasted on macaroni, tomato soup and falso
cheese cooked at three hundred fifty degrees
which I called spaghetti until I was twenty-one
and loved our nights there, Thelma, Libby, and Ida,
fat as I was then, fat and near-sighted
and given over to art, such as I saw it,
though smothered somewhat by the three of them;
and it would be five years of breaking loose,
reading Kropotkin first, then reading Keats,
and standing on my head and singing by which
I developed the longing, though I never
turned against that spaghetti, I was always
loyal to one thing, you could almost measure
my stubbornness and my wildness by that loyalty.

FLUTE

Since there was nothing going up or down I sat
against the wall and listened to her phrases,
her doing the same thing over and over, returning
endlessly to get it right, her cats
probably not listening for all I know
her lips freezing, and softly she counted and must have
nodded once for out of those finger holes
the argument was for spring since there were onions
growing outside in the cracks and I had to move
my legs two times against my will and I had to
open my eyes and interrupt my singing.

LOVE

A part of me eats her fingers and a part of me
soaks the dishes but I hate to be scattered
for that is why it took so long and with my
hands enbubbled like that it's up to her
mostly and I resist for I have the counter
still to scrub and I have a wet
dish towel in my hand as we walk up
eleven steps to the landing followed by six
for in the latter part of my life I'm counting
and nothing, nothing, is sweeter than her protest
or mine, for we are protestants and lie there
hours on end protesting, that is love,
in her house and mine, both the same except that
I have two sets of stairs, a front and a back,
so counting is endless, at least it's multiple,
and you know multiple and what it goes with.

What if Merwin and Collins bent down to smell
the licorice and the butterflies still weren't moving—
or he got off a train in Trenton, his cane
in one hand and a bottle of wine in the other
and he had an apron in his bag and two quarts of
sauce to weigh it down and he would argue
with Anne Marie about the sugar though those two
never met; and what if it was a question
of not just chopped-up carrots for a sweetcner
but crushing the tomatoes and removing
the bitter seeds; and there was somebody else
I can't remember at the table, but he was
I know an expert on Horace and it came down to
what the Romans ate for breakfast since out of
just those facts we argued and sometimes the argument
soared—the argument soaring, isn't that one
of the definitions? Horace believed in soaring—
that is my own word though you could argue
the other way around, that Horace never
soared—or even plunged—and as for Bill Matthews
and how he soared, you only had to hear him
praise the turnips and the unwashed sea urchins
or watch his heart break open with regret
and biting self-reproach to know how he did.

Since it was birdseed and plates of water and leftovers
and there was nothing going up or down I sat
against the fence underneath my maple and listened
to thunder, for starters, and since where I lived there wasn't
a flute for miles I did without though I will
never quit being shocked at the stops, how music
comes from holes, including darkness and light,
and joy and gloom; and I have come to honor my
fence above the others for it is a chain-link and
in its way it *modulates*, the fences both
left and right they hardly do and dogwood
is out now, here and there, mine has a skirt
and it will blossom for a week, it's like a
bush more than a tree but it contains
the same dark bloody history and the redbud
too and even the locust, and if you
live long enough you will die knowing it.

STOMACHS

Some technical matter, something about stomachs,
the number of them, that or the size of them,
while something that hovers above which could be in birds
and no place else sounds in the background, suffering
maybe, maybe pleasure, the wing
and the beak different except in one gray speckled
specimen where whistling—in both cases—
is almost the same, and rising I whistle for I am
doomed to imitate everything and whether the
whistling was the same it's hard to tell
for I was speckled too, in both cases.

BEFORE EATING

Here's to your life
and here's to your death

and here's to coughing
and here's to breath.

Here's to snowfall
here's to flurry,

here's your hat,
what's your hurry?

Here's to judge,
here's to Jewry,

here's to beer
here's to brewery.

Leave me alone,
I want to worry;

make me lamb chops,
make me curry.

Here's to Voigt,
here's to Bidart,

here's getting off
to a running start.

Here's to Dove,
here's to Levine,

here's to the graveyards
in Berlin and Wien.

Here's to Gilbert
who learned it from me,

here's to the ninety-foot
Christmas tree

he fell on his head from
shortening his height,

here's to the grimness
of his grim night;

and I could go on for
forty pages,

listing my joys
and listing my rages,

but I should stop
while I'm still ahead

and make my way
to my own crooked bed;

so here's to the end,
the final things,

and here's to forever
and what that brings,

and here's to a cup of
coffee in the winter

and here's to the needle,
and here's to the splinter.

And here's to the pear tree
I couldn't live without,

and here's to its death
I wrote about

from 1966
to 1972,

a kind of root
from which I grew,

and here's to the fruit—
I like that too,

bruised and juicy
through and through,

and here's to the core
oh most of all

and how I chewed it
from Mall to Mall

and how I raddled
the stem in my teeth

as if it were wind
against a red leaf;

and here's to the wind
and here's to your eyes

and here's to their honey,
dark as the skies

and here's to the silk roof
over your head

and here's to the pillows
and here's to the bed

and here's to your plaid robe,
and here's to your breast,

and here's to your new coat
and here's to your vest

and your fine mind and its desire,
as wild and crazy as the fire

we saw burning going home in the dark,
driving by and wanting to park,

but stopped by sirens and flashing lights—
wild nights, wild nights,

a pine tree in the other lane,
cones exploding in my brain.

Part II

He was dead so he was only a puff
of smoke at the most and I had to labor to see him
or just to hear and when we spoke it was as
if we were waiting in the rain together
or in a shelter on 96th street or by the
side of a train in Washington, D.C., say,
changing engines and patting each others' stomachs
by way of intimacy, and he said what he
wanted most of all, when it came to trains,
was merely to stand on the platform looking out
the dirty window at the water beyond
the row of houses or the stand of trees
for it was *distance* he loved now and the smell of
the ocean, even more than coffee, but it was
only *concoction* for he didn't have the senses
anymore, and I forgot to say that
he was a veteran and he wore a green cap
that had KOREA VETERAN printed on the face
with three bright battle ribbons below the lettering,
and I forgot to say his ears were large,
the way it sometimes happens in older men,
though he was dead, and he was on the train with
his wife who had red hair of sorts and a dress
that spread out like a tassel of silk, and war

was what we talked about and what the flowers
were the way a poppy was the emblem
of World War One and we both laughed at how
there were no flowers for Korea nor any
poems for that matter though he was sad and although
he wore the hat he said it was a stupid
useless war, unlike Achilles Odysseus
talked to in Hell, who loved his war and treasured
the noses he severed and the livers he ruptured,
and picture them selling their asphodel in front of
a supermarket or a neighborhood bank
and picture us waiting until our ears were long
just to hate just one of their dumb butcheries.

JACKKNIFE

Sitting here watching the other side of the glass,
some paper flower heads, some orange and red berries,
practicing starvation, that and getting ready
to pour my milk, starting again to study
my other life and how I carried a key
wherever I went and how it was the key
and not the five-dollar bill and the loose change
in my left pants pocket and not the wallet with one
rotten permission inside, a *license*, and how
I never lost that key and it was large
and thick the way they made them then, I all
but wore it smooth, bronze paint over iron,
tin under nickel, it was what I trusted
since in my county, what was there, aside from
the great beauty it was only destruction,
deer eating the poison leaves and gases
exploding here and there—you wouldn't think
a key would make the difference or a brand-new
knife in the leather pocket of a boot
when George was king and Hoover president.

Not that the swan was good to me, not that
she had pity on my pauvre attempts
at swimming without a bladder nor that she
would help me with my spelling nor would read me
the words I couldn't see or she would tell me
how what to do or even how to tie my
tie or button my shirt or what to wear
or that she let me float with her without
reaching over to break my neck for which I
hated her or I was just uncomfortable
at all that beak in the air, that eye in the sky,
that curved neck, and she was brutal when it
came to water rights, and it was the black
between her eyes and her mouth I hated most
although I'm sure she loved it herself, and in the
old ponds I ate my vegetables
and reached my neck up for the irrigation;
and such it was that I was despised, or was I
only ignored? and what does a perfect feather
mean among those waterfowl? and love for
my own lagoon drove me you poor bastards
that oh your babies I almost loved I almost
treasured them, what more, what new delectables?

The very thing I was trying not to see was
so close to my nose that I couldn't see anything
else, and I had to rely on a stranger to
distinguish one thing from another, and
on one occasion the edges were smoking so
and the smoke crawled to the middle in such a way
that I had to depend on smoke alone, and fog,
and clouds and steam and such to light the way,
nor did I even know the day, or the month,
nor what caused smoke to come from manholes though
temperature was my guess and gusts of wind,
and snow on the river is always my guess though any
sudden change will do and sometimes filth
alone, and as for cracking that comes in
March and sometimes even earlier and,
as we used to say, two sticks exploding
by one just touching the other or two black clouds
crashing into each other and two brass cymbals
clashing; and on the stage of the old Casino,
the burlesque house on Diamond Street I spent
my tenth grade in, one of the dancers grinding
to a drum or the drum to her, or in a show
of force my mother popping her gum, or as a
symbol of rapture lost, though it is weird

even to think of it now, and also to show
contempt for any rapture and to make you
burn cynical, he of the baggy pants,
in double time, with a fake nose, with shoes
three sizes too large, a pillow for glut, he mimics
her steps, oh lovable horror, his paper whistle
crawling up her thigh, his stogie exploding.

WHAT THEN?

You know I know there is just enough light
between the boards and that the tree creaked and
the branches scraped against the roof, and all I
can think about is whether my shoes will be covered
with dust when all is said and done or whether
the cake will cover it and cracked and brittle
they rise once again as all shoes rise
both high and dry if even the tongue is split,
and what was called a leather top was loose
from its moorings; you know the pain the shoe
itself swelling can cause here, how can we rid
the world of swelling, that was my first grievance,
or muck to start with, muck was the problem, no one
I know should die but what do my two black shoes
know, let's say a creature will blow them dry
by beating his wings or let's say we'll walk next time
say north instead of south, oh nearer my face
to thee and nearer your face to me, what then?

As if one poet then who was in his sixties
I wanted to tell him that I read his book
and how I lingered on one page and couldn't
go to the next, I had to read it again,
and later I kissed it, but I couldn't tell him that
nor did I ever write, since I lost his
letter, I remember putting it in
my inside pocket with the colored pens
and how it must have slipped out as I ran
down the four steps and over the forsythia
looking for my keys; and at the annual
ceremonies somewhere close I think to
Gramercy Park he barked at me not knowing
how much I loved his work nor did he see
out of the dusty window left of the cloakroom
how a dog had severed the head of a pigeon
and how its bloody feathers lay on the sidewalk
and blood was on the dog's round face and how
oddly he growled and how he licked his lips.

DREAM III

I would like to live on air too
and I have an idea the kind of nourishment
I'd get with or without my strings for what did
I need them for and all those gnarled roots
beside the wilted rhododendron and what did
I need the dried-out grapes for and the wet
leaves and one harmonica under a rusted
burst-out water pipe and even a mangled
sparrow under the porch the way my brain works.

This I learned from Angela, a fawn's
ass has to be clean or he won't shit,
and if there is no mother to lick him, you have
to use toilet paper, lovingly, this way
you become his mother, you get to name him
and get to find him on Johnson Road, a '74
Mercury heating up beside him, the owner
in tears, and you, the mother, consoling *him*
as you both drag the body into the woods
which keeps you calm although your hands are shaking
and you are breathing hard from pushing the one
remaining leg into the ground without
disturbing the bloated stomach or the nose
that wants to stick out of the leaves nor do you
lower the shovel and flatten the ground
for you have babied the universe and you walk
with fear—or care—you walk with care—and wipe
your face with dirt and kiss the murderer.

Wasn't it refreshing then and there to
find a Red Goose shoe where there had been
a feather only a day or two before?
And wasn't it a lark to walk across
a makeshift wooden bridge above the noisy
wall of water above the debris? And how
did a shoe get there, and was it a miracle
or was it an accident that there in the very
place where the egg was hatched and the feather was dropped
a shoe by that very name took the place of a bird,
and was it too tight or too loose, and was it leather
or was it cardboard, how long would it take to tell you?

More than anything else it was
the smell of dead birds that overpowered
you as you walked into that woods
and everything else was sheer bullshit
including the violets you picked in the openings
and tied in small bouquets holding
your nose withal as if you truly
had someone to give a posy to, and there
was either a wolf or there wasn't, it doesn't matter
now, for it was second or third growth,
and it was more scrag than not and anyhow
it's house to house now ugly fucking streets
where once da da da da and you were beautiful
innocent young though you were fat and clumsy
too but you were you and you treasured the blue nosegay.

LORCA

The fact that no one had ever seen Lorca run
had only to do with the legend of his clumsiness
for one foot was shorter than the other and he was
terrified to cross the street by himself,
though dogs barking in the mountains above him
brought him back to his senses and caused him
when he was alone to try leaping and skipping
the way you did; and he tried the hop, skip, and jump
he learned from the 1932 Olympics
and loaded the left side of his mouth with green tobacco
when he was only eleven for he took comfort
in every form of degradation; and it was
in John Jay Hall in 1949
that Geraldo from Pittsburgh made a personal connection
for they were both housed in room 1231
twenty years apart not counting the months,
and only one of them heard Eisenhower give his maiden
    speech
outside the courtyard entrance, and there were bitter
oranges enough for them both, and you can imagine
one of our poets in the hands of our own bastards,
but what is the use of comparing, only the hats
are different—though I'm not too sure—the roses
maybe they stuffed in our mouths—the Granadas.

A visit with Muriel in her New York apartment,
helping her into the kitchen, making her tea,
freeing her from a statement but she knew it
by heart and wouldn't listen though there was a
rupture somewhere in the second sentence,
and we were alone for an hour until her nurse
came back and scolded her for leaving her bed
and sitting with only a loosely knitted shawl
over her shoulders and only a thin slip
to cover her, a silk or rayon; and when
the subject was murder and lying, there was a look of
abandonment to her as it was when she let
her poems fall on the floor in Philadelphia
in the long narrow theater on Walnut Street
but I never finished *my* tea and I escaped
before the nurse could get to me and I
turned west, for the record, near Lexington, I think,
against the sun, for it was March already.

Sometimes he is mustard and sometimes blue,
sometimes it is slicing and cutting and sometimes
it's only rain that brings him to the surface
and he does it to keep the robin company,
and there is a heavy smell for those who live too
close to the earth and if there is no brain
or if it is dispersed and thence divided
he is only eaten the more and isn't it
a joy that there is no light and he has to look
elsewhere for his doom and his nostalgia.

As for those who face their death by wind
and call it by the weird name of forgiveness
they alone have the right to marry birds,
and those who stopped themselves from falling down
by holding the wall up or the sink in place
they can go without much shame for they
have lived enough and they can go click, click
if they want to, they can go tok, tok
and they can marry anything, even hummingbirds.

LOVE BOX

Because of the Paganini I lifted the lid
the minute I got back from Prague and kissed
the two ridiculous inlaid hearts that were
located so carefully and lacquered so well
they could have been painted on, and I would have said
one was me and one was you and you were
standing beside a column that propped the roof up
and you said "Don't forget, I saved your life once"
and I said, "I'll never forget," and there were walls
plated in bronze and dogs of gold and silver,
except the machine broke down, or what it did,
the music just ended, or just when you thought it did
there was another *ping*; and I got up
to put my white shirt on I wear to buy
my carrots in and I rewound the box
though it was June and there was blood on my fingers
from strawberries and I examined the tiny
pins reaching up from the comb and the block of wood
to see where music comes from and to learn
once and for all how feeling is converted,
though we were in a boat in Naples harbor—
I like that better—and we were floating and there was
more than an inch of water and the inlaid
hearts were shaking and the pins were going wild.

He had more than one white shirt
and two pairs of pants instead of one,
and once in New York he crawled inside a taxi
for diabetes was making him weak,
and when he reached the corner of Eighth and Bowery
he slid into a corner for his friends
were everywhere, and though he hated the meter
he also hated the conversation in Urdu
the driver was having with his wife or daughter,
for he wanted some silence, or maybe he wanted
a little attention for all that money and not
to be ignored this way; and when the cab
stopped to let him off he suffered the new
trick of evening it off to the highest dollar
and felt halfway justified in stiffing him
but gave him two thin bills though the rigid
security wall made it impossible
to leave with grace, and this is how he entered
the open space beside the School of the Arts
and struggled for understanding in front of the pillars
downstairs Abe Lincoln himself had once ignited.

Rose in your teeth, my darling, rose in your teeth,
and blood on your hands and shoes on your feet,
and barefoot in mud and how the shoes went floating
on bodies of water, I sold them at Baker's and Burt's
and carried the boxes on high; and there were women
galore who sat there in rows in their chairs on their thrones
in stockings of silk, and we rolled by on wagons of wood
and counted till midnight in codes and by numbers and
    letters,
and I did the forms though once I led the charge
and I was the priest for two or three hours; and there were
forgotten styles in colors you couldn't imagine
and heels of the past and folded tongues and such,
and I was hungry at one in the morning and ate
forgotten foods, and can't you tell how I
was a woman then and ransacked the upper shelves
and how I ran for the money and remembered
twelve to fourteen numbers and I knew
the stock and detested the manager and kept
my own tallies and ate my sandwich from a bag
during the later days of the war and just after,
when there were murder gardens everywhere.

When it comes to girls the Chihuahua
on Ninth Street going down to
Washington on the left side
below the Hong Kong Fruit,
he knows where he's going, between their
beautiful legs, his eyes
bulge a little, his heart,
because he is small, surges,
explodes too much, he is
erotic, his red tongue
is larger than a squirrel's, but
not too much, nor does he
walk on a wire with fresh
ricotta in his mouth nor
an apple they sell for a quarter,
a bit of rot on one side but
sweet underneath the skin, more
Macintosh than not, he
loves Velveeta, he knows
the price of bananas, he whines
when there is a death; there was one
drowning in a sewer,
his owner gave me five dollars
for lifting the lid with a hammer

and going down into the muck
when I was twelve, it was
my first act of mercy
and she gave me a towel
that matched the Chihuahua's towel
and ah he trembled containing
such knowledge and such affection
and licked my face and forced me
to shut my eyes, it was
so much love, his whole
body was shaking and I,
I learned from him and I
learned something once from a bird
but I don't know his name
though everyone I tell it to
asks me what his name was
and it is shameful, what
was he, a dog? The Klan
was flourishing all the while
we dreamed of hydroelectric
so we were caught in between
one pole and another and
we were Hegelian or just
Manichean, we kept

the hammer on top of the manhole
so we could lift it to get
our soft balls and tennis balls
though he who weighed a pound
could easily fall into
the opening, such was our life
and such were our lives the last
few years before the war when
there were four flavors of ice cream
and four flavors only; I'll call him
Fatty; I'll call him Peter;
Jésus, I'll call him, but only
in Spanish, with the "h" sound,
as it is in Mexico;
Jésus, kiss me again,
Jésus, you saved *me*,
Jésus, I can't forget you;
and what was her name who gave me
the towel? and who was I?
and what is love doing in
a sewer, and how is disgrace
blurred now, or buried?

Part III

Introduction to "The Preacher"

In the King James version of the book of Ecclesiastes, the self-announced speaker is one who calls himself—in the very first line—the Preacher, but this title, which maybe sets the wrong tone, does not appear in the original Hebrew. My use of it as *my* title is mostly an ironic continuation. Also the word "vanity" (all is vanity) is a wildly distant and inexact translation of the Hebrew *havel*, which could more appropriately be translated "mist," "fog," "wind," or even "emptiness," which has a very modern ring to it. In the Jewish Publication Society translation according to the traditional Hebrew text (the Tanakh), the word is translated as "futility," which is even wider—in spirit—from the mark, though it may be more literal (all is futility).

It was in reading Alicia Ostriker's provocative and insightful essay on Ecclesiastes that I was reminded of this. I thank her, as I do Willis Barnstone, Rabbi Sandy Roth Parrion, Chard deNiord, Chris Hedges, Arthur Vogelsang, Jeremiah Ostriker, Ira Sadoff, and Tony Hoagland for their help.

The poem, in a way, belongs to Peter Richards as much as it does to me. I thank Peter for his receptiveness, his memory, his ideas, his humor, and for the words he wrote in response to my initial lines and first tentative ideas.

I have taken a hundred liberties, as my pencil has directed, and have concocted a romance and a comedy and shuffled time, and listened only to the wings. I thank the wings and I apologize to everyone else.

63

As if the one tree you love so well and hardly
can embrace it is so huge so that with-
out it there might be a hole in the universe
explains how the killing of any one thing can
likewise make a hole except that without
its existence there was neither a hole nor not a hole
I said to my friend Peter and after he left
I walked to the tree again and put my arms
around the trunk or almost did for I was
embracing it preparatory should I say
to its dying for it was one of the many
dying trees along my river mainly
sycamore and locust—

                              you must tire I
said to Peter always hearing the same
trees sung the same words singing, the same
heart breaking I said and *con permissione*
I will change trees though I am almost eighty
now, but what the hell, there probably are
others along the river, though there was a point
when social security was kicking in I didn't
go to the palms nor did I go to Boca
to traffic in herons nor did I go to Miami

where my people walk around in scary
black suits and hats perched over their other hats
just in case and just in case nor did I
go to California nor stay in Iowa nor
buy a farmhouse in the Pioneer Valley
south of Brattleboro, thanks God, thanks God—

and Peter interrupts me remembering a
squirrel in Iowa that bit all the daisies,
a mad squirrel of sorts but *certes* no madder
than our own hot shots with their squirrel rifles killing
squirrels from two miles up at wedding parties
of all things, of all things—

                              and that's what you
mean by a hole in the universe, isn't it? Peter
asks and he remembers the garden we built
and what we planted, how I went to the Kmart
and bought the cardboard planters and plastic trays
and how we built a fence—give way to groundhogs
ye black potatoes and brown tomatoes, and ah
the railroad ties there planted in gravel and it
was a hole *he* dug—I came home one day and
he was into it up to his knees—

                              and Peter is
tall, and he remembers the cosmos, I the
delphiniums, but both of us hated that squirrel,
eating a daisy on the highest limb of
my apple tree, the one that died, and she just
laughing and giving us the finger, and on my
cell phone he remembers how we drove to
the kingdom of used lawn mowers, I on the way
yelling out the window to every mower
of hill and valley, how much will you take for
that lawn mower, that lawn mower, for
there *is* progress, *n'est-ce pas*, isn't there
Peter, I used to hate green grass but now I
almost adore it, and what about the holes in
Europe and Asia I ask—

                         what of the holes in
this or that heart, he says—

                              I say repair it!

He says, and are you going to plant a Berber,
clever of hand, to cut the colored marble
and know how it looks a distance of five miles

66

as in that notebook you scratch away with your black
and red ballpoint you are so proud of, just like
the Berber chipping away knowing in your knuckles
what it will look like when it's finished, each scratch
critical though it's not as if you were writing
by the laws of Plato—perish the thought—it is
what it is—and you will look at it, you and me,
and say "that's right," not even, "that's what I had
in mind," for it is your knuckles that write, still blessed
by suppleness, if not your hips, if not
your knees, God bless your knees, God bless the cartilage,
God bless the ligaments—you with your hole in the universe,
so weird and extreme.

Peter says this, and he
and I trail off and since he gave me a tape
of Leonard Cohen with a voice so deep it shook
my red Honda, I thought therein did it lie,
something about Vienna, something Brooklyn,
her torn blue raincoat—or his—I can't get the gender
right, the facts don't add up, it's *Jane* and it rhymes
with Lili Marlene, that famous lamppost, the same
nostalgia, his song or hers, Peter loves the turn
and does his preacherly voice, we have just half

a minute or so to talk and throw sentences
at one another, "no one knows what it means,"
that is his favorite, "no one can understand it,"
"we walk around in a fog," *I* say that,
"and live in a mist," "we are in a Russian
sweat house, climbing the bleachers, breathing pure steam."
"It's like the smoke," he says, "in a Chinese painting,
there are the mountains and there is the hut you'll live in,
you barely can see the trees in the little gorge
left side of the hut, the green intense,
the tops of fir trees almost touching the steep
broken path;" "it's like living in a cloud,"
I say, "though the sun is shining, whatever that
means, when you're healthy and money in your pocket,
and walking five miles an hour by your favorite
body of water it's hard to remember the cloud,
you are so sure of yourself."

      "What made you think
of a hole the way you did?" he asks.

       "My figures
always start with the literal and the spreading

is like blood spreading," I say, "and as for the wound it
comes from growing up with coal, the murder
of everything green, rivers burning, cities
emptied, humans herded, the vile thinking
of World War I and II, the hole in England,
the hole in Germany, and what we can't en-
dure, the hole in Japan, Truman, the third
assistant baker's helper, he should pick at
his harp in Hell; when I read about
Tamurlane, say, and how he piled up the heads,
and David and the Moabites, he made them
lie down to see who was longer or shorter and put
half of them to death, it had to do with
ropes, he may have piled up skulls for all
I know, and Samuel the prophet loved him to pieces,
and Hernán Cortés and Genghis Kahn, but also,
I hate to say it, private Sharon, pig
Ariel, and the Lebanese jaunt, a massacre,
as I remember—let's not forget the names,
Sabra and Shatila"—

                        "It's justice you want,
isn't it?" quoth Peter.

"I'll tell you what,
(I say) when I see a hairy vine encircle a
tree and make its red mark on the life sap
gushing desperately into the forementioned leaves I
even sigh then let alone when a duck is pulled
into the water, oh let alone when the pig
'allowed' the Christian militia to clean up
the Arab families by murdering them, by which
as a Jew I lost any slight righteousness,
never mind keeping score, or I just remember
Mark Twain on the Spanish War, *Betrayal*
Americanus, start anywhere, a Moro
village in the Philippines, say, six hundred
unarmed nonwhites massacred in Sand Creek—
that was an Indian village in Colorado—
same thing, I'm sorry I'm so obscure—you know
about the garbage men in Memphis, guess what
make the three cars are they put in the spaces
underneath King's balcony—am I
boring you?"

            "We spent the summer arguing
all about form," he says, "there was an anthology

that kept us going, you raged like a lion raging
after his seventh nap, hunger sets in then,
it lies someplace below the lungs and water
heavy with salt come out of the glands in back of
the dripping tongue—it was an argument
without sides, both of us sing."

                                    "I remember
now—an army of doctors in white coats
bent over a frog, or each of them had a frog,
and they were concentrating on the stomach
(I say) and what it ate yesterday, making
frog noises while they worked—they croaked
together, sort of, though every once in a while
there was a loud single mournful sound
that had a frog-like beauty about it I listened
to as if I were in the sedges or lying
down on the green stones beside a green,
mucky, and fly-drenched pond and I knew who
the king of that pond was and in spite of the croaking,
given my allegiance was to warblers
and birds of that sort, I once in a while sighed
in recognition of the sound."

"That summer," he
said, "I would have asked which side of the pond was
better for swimming. Do you remember the heat? Form
itself was dissolved, we all turned to waves, the sun
beat down on our glasses, we couldn't even touch the weeds,
Immanuel Kant was trapped in the bulrushes
screaming for ice, form was the bucket, it stood there
tilting a little on a rock, it was
inside the bucket, and sloshing, give it three days
and it would evaporate, it would return,
as form always does, to air."

"I was still struggling
to free the poem," I said, "to free the poet,
buckets sound good to me, Immanuel Kant sounds
good, Schiller sounds better. I shouldn't be spending my
time doing this, the only point is releasing
the tongue; there was a man who cut his own arm
off to free himself, the fox in his trap
thus gnaws himself loose, and that is what you should do
for that is form, and he who was the preacher,
how did he free himself? how did he loosen
his tongue?"

        "I don't think cutting his arm off," Peter
said, "and why did you say I had a preacherly
voice?"

        "I only was thinking about the preacher,
he who called himself preacher (I said), one of my
rabbis, a Reconstructionist I think she
was, said he was the first person in the
Bible to have a *name*, that is to have
a proper name, in Hebrew, which makes no sense
considering Samuel, Saul, David, Moses,
Joshua, Miriam, Amos, Ruth, Esther,
unless we are referring to a less than
mythical person, someone out of a telephone
book, Davis MacIntyre, James McFadden, Slavian Rosskies,
though he is not even mentioned in King James,
putting a new wrinkle on the literal,
the dull folk I hate so well, the hell-
bathers nodding their sawdust heads above,
or in the best-case scenario inside,
that heated lake so they could be tormented
day and night forever and ever for there is a
book, you know, and teenage boys in cheap
blue suits to write it down, I saw them knocking

on the front doors in my own neighborhood,
only they were wearing green sunglasses
the way the police did on early TV
with clipboards in their hands, who, for the sake
of a lamb, condemn all dogs and sorcerers,
read it yourself."

            "From what I read," said Peter,
"preacher was an accountant, he was a scribe
from the third century before the lamb,
and I might add it wasn't just sorcerers,
but liars and murderers as well, which puts
a different face on it."

                        "There is a ring
of modernity to the word 'liar,' " I said,
"it is, after all, our greatest contribution
and what we do best, better than murder I think
though we are good at both—my Bible" (I said)
"I'm just reminding you—has God exploding
inside his mountain just before he gives
Moses the two white slabs—I can't read it
without thinking about the movie, I saw it

in Easton P.A. in 1973,
the day before they tore the theater down
on Third Street to make room for a parking lot,
as part of the Destruction; it was a fake
Moroccan from 1925 with painted
statues and cold-forged Spanish steel I stole
out of the dumpster for my own steel banister
and it was a Sunday, the very last day, I saw
Charlton Heston with his arm raised up and
female angels blowing trumpets for the bored
Sunday School classes, all of whose teachers had thrown
their gold earrings into a pile since they
loved golden calves the more, the mountain was smoking
and there was lightning and thunder as only befitted
a place like that and thick darkness, the word was
'thick,' and there was room for nine cars—
a hole all right"—

                    "I love the details," said Peter,
"God as a lawyer, what we should do with the fat
at a sacrifice, what you can sing or not sing"—

"Mostly what you can eat," I said.

"I never
saw the movie," said Peter, "though what I'm taken
with on the one hand is the flower eaten
and what of civilization it may trigger
and who was the squirrel in this and what did his color
signify, if anything, and were his
holes holes and what did they harbor, and was your
love of trees, especially that of the sycamore,
more justly the love of women, didn't I myself
wander as you did and find, as I wrote, an eighteenth-
century 'grove of beauty' inside of which
was a 'true cognitive woman fully naked,
fully alive'—can I quote myself?—and
'sexually outgoing and philosophically wild.' "

"I love those lines," I said "and later on
you mention 'spheres,' you're thinking of planets, I know,
but my mind turns to Borges and his essay
on Blaise Pascal's abyss rabbi Barnstone
says is a type of the hole, and you use 'hair,'
the *word* hair, to describe the branches thick
with leaves and we are back in the world of poetry
though I keep thinking of the weeping willow
that also died halfway between my back

porch and the garden I watched going bald
year after year until there was nothing left
but a few strands, you might say patches, an ugliness
I didn't know what to do with, I just stared
at it day after day"—

                    "I like the apple trees
up against the lilacs," Peter said,
"near the alley; you didn't know they were good
for eating, what with the worms, and the bulges, they were
the sweetest apples I ever tasted, it was a
taste we lost somewhere—in one of my stanzas
I say 'there is no single atom in the yard
our conversation would agree on' and I
write about you 'forever taking a rest
after planting only one row'—I'm taking it
out of context (he says), I think 'holes,'
is what was lying in back of my mind, there has to
always be something there, a phrase, an idea, a
person even, or a mood or a kind of
shadow, different poets do it differently—
I guess what I'm saying is obvious—I thought
of holes with eyes, a hole with hands, a hole
of holes for the squirrel which when I have it acting

like a mole, it brings up Alice, mole in a hole,
nor should you miss my reference to Augustine—
'a kind of fall,' I said, referring to the hex,
making the red squirrel momentous though I'm wrecking
my poem this way"—

                    "How did it happen," I said,
"we started to talk about the preacher? Why
do I always get dragged into a subject I have to
labor over as if I were planting cantaloupes
in stone or salt and struggling with the dried-up
fruit, a watering can in one hand, burned-down
shit in the other, and also up a hill and
in the lateral roots of one or another of
two dead trees, or choosing in the garbage
between a coal and a potato, or planting
tomatoes in a pool of water, how did it
happen that was my land, where was my mule,
my wise mule?"

          "It was a song," said Peter,
"and one thing led to another; you were listening to
Charles Mingus, 'Ecclusiastics,' either

because you liked the music or liked the spelling
and that was how you got started, explaining what was
vanity and what it wasn't and what the word in
Hebrew was and how your Bible said
'futility,' and that was worse, and 'fog' was
the word you used and 'it was Buddha' you shouted
under your dead apple, now you're doing it
because of your new rabbi, if you had only
listened to 'Eat That Chicken.' "

                       "The word is wind,"
I said, "more than fog. Though there is a hint
of water, maybe vapor—that is where I
saw it—that is where I started to see
things differently; there was one sentence that governed
everything and I have studied that sentence
for six months now, it gives me peace just as it
frightens me, the preacher says it or someone
who calls himself the preacher, you may have a better
word for it (I say to Peter) everything is
lost when mouths speak, look at the fog,
look at the fog, or maybe he just speaks the
odd words from his own village, a certain

haze on the horizon, say, but that may
be the park where the squirrels play, or the frog
opens his mouth and keeps it open"—

                                        "I know
the sentence," says Peter, "it has the word 'eternity'
in it, am I right? although one village
speaks differently than another and some of us
after we hear the word have to sit down;
it has a bit of physics in it, a bit of
philosophy, that's how it was, that's how it
is maybe."

                    "For eternity," I said, "it
could have said the age of the world, or just
'world,' that's what you find in the top drawer
of the nightstand at all the chain hotels
although in the second drawer it says 'hole'
and in the Book of Angels buried behind the
stationery it says 'Cloud of Fire'
although eternity is a tricky word
depending how you look at it but what the
lesson is is you don't know and stop
trying, though that might be the joyous part,

that trying, having no knowledge and living
imperfectly, just being an animal
whose grasp exceeds his greed, whose jaw his feed,
whose nose extends beyond his wildest dream,
that is sadness, right?"

                    "That itself is a hole,"
said Peter, "I'd call it a hole."

                              "It was a gift,"
I said, "even to have it for a minute,
someone I know calls it a consolation, the
grub crawling across my kitchen table
by pulling and pushing holds up his tiny green head
and sniffs the air or dances back and forth
to get his knowledge, the front of his body, the front
third of his body is in the air."

                         "My head
is green too," said Peter, "What happened to Arthur?"

"Sir Arthur," I said, "he's one of my rabbis, and throws
a baseball farther than anyone I know—
or used to know—or used to throw—he says

there is no end or beginning so how can it have
a hole, or how can we know if it has a hole,
nor does it have a structure, he says, or what
we call a structure, world without end; Jeremiah,
Alicia's husband, he of the stars, most dear
and generous Jeremiah, we sat down
in black T-shirts on Nassau Street in Princeton
discussing the universe, only he *knew* and I
might as well be chewing a pencil, he liked
the fact that everything was mist, he said
he didn't know about eternity but
as for holes it was the human presence,
if anything that made them, in the sense
that I was using the word, but of course he thought
at first I meant black holes and he was kind, we
never talked about New York or Dresden,
we never said craters or cups or excavations,
or filthy places or hiding places or pits, say,
or trenches or caves or cellars or sinkholes or hellholes"—

"That leaves the bucket," Peter said, "and water
sloshing, and it should be cloudy or soapy, a
soup some people call it, some people a tea,
and I already said Immanuel Kant cooked

that tea and you agreed 'Kant and Schiller' is
what you said, but if I turn the bucket
over I have a *drum*, and I can start with
fingers or palms, I hold it between my knees
it's always held like that—and it was tilted,
as everything is tilted."

       "Kant," I said, "was
probably not; the one most boring thing
we know is that the hauswives in Königsberg
could tell the time by where he was walking, at ten
in the morning, he passed his first tavern—what I
long for more than anything else is a speech
not tilted, it breaks my heart that I
grew up in darkness so, I have a kind of
remorse for it, absurd as it sounds, and you will
have to forgive my vengeance, what I learned
I learned with a vengeance."

       "It comes out as anger,"
quoth Peter, "you can rage."

       "It comes from listening
to music," I said, "it comes from watching a horse being

beaten in Philadelphia, it's all because of
the clock in my head, it's like the air conditioner
sitting on my attic floor, and more than
that, the frog has descended on my river
and merely opened his mouth, a form of eating
detestable, I can't stop talking about his
mouth, although we eat him, we frogs, and snails
they eat a hundred ways, some extend their
thin noses into the mouths of shells they
share the water with and some just curve their
long tongues here and there and scrape; in *my* water,
the largemouth bass and snapping turtles vie
for ducklings, starting with legs, the dinner *reversus*
for fowl comes after fish and thus the prophet
mourned and dreamed of hay but Mingus, Lord Mingus,
he taught us again to eat that chicken, oh yeah,
but no one thought of sleep deprivation and boring
holes in the head and sucking out information—

and walking back from the wooden bridge above
the lumberyard that curved underneath the iron
rails a few yards south I saw, oh yeah,
a polished branch free of the bushes I thought
was a dead fox it lay on its side so,

with one leg up and its mouth open that death
relieved it just as death does, we are relieved
and lie on our side or our backs; and polished branches
everywhere and in the coffins and in the
rivers and heaped in ravines the way my cousins
were in Europe but to my joy my tree
was still standing and I had forgotten how thick
it was, I calculated by hand, though it meant
diving into the poison ivy, buckets,
buckets, were everywhere, Mingus trapped his
frogs that way and Kant his—right or wrong—
his liberation of the senses, given
Königsberg that way and when I walked
my two miles, my two or three miles, and ended,
for I ended, at one of my white wooden bridges
I traveled freely, past and future, though if it
wasn't for the pain in my shoulder blades
I might not have thought about it and got there—
surprise!—in twenty seconds, in no time flat, the
way it was when I ran, the way it was
bouncing a ball, walking through a wet forest,
and it is circles I love in spite that I walk
in a line beginning at catnip, ending at loosestrife,
and catnip is blue, its flowers are blue and the bees

they purr, they scratch up sofas, they stink up my porch,
but most of all they stretch afterwards and yawn
only to distract you, time was such
that I was distracted, I was in front of the catnip
then, I hope I wasn't deluded, for I was
in time *myself*, I couldn't see to see and
it was *now* that ruined me, now I was ruined,
both now and then, and now and then, and only
through *thinking* could I escape, only by staring,
and only sometimes, in front of catnip, since time it
waits for no one and at my back I hear and
I wrote love letters in the sand and time
after time my heart was young and gay and flies
in time and time flies and fugit fugit and
I have clarified and deepened my thought
even though I was in time at least a
little and there must be a mystery
that governs it and we are in it too deep
to understand or *verbalize* it and I am
stupid at mathematics and Lord God knows
what I said unwittingly and I go
down to Nassau Street to beg the florist
for forgiveness and the donkey who sits in the jazzy
police wagon and I'll say this . . ."

"That donkey
is underpaid just like the rest of us,"
quoth Peter, "and he resents the doctor of time
who, if he knew what you said, would laugh at you,
wearing his khakis, wearing his glasses on the tip
of his nose, holding them on with a ribbon, drinking
his tall coffee at Starbucks, his right hand
thinking this is an absolute after all,
and what is an *adjective*, he probably counts
steps like you do, he probably counts to a hundred
in intervals of fifty, or twenty, prolonging the
pain even as he tries to reduce it unless he's
playing handball or making love . . ."

"I want to
disappear too," I said, "though that's not the word,
the word is 'appear,' and I walked the path from the
lumberyard north to the goose farm on my right and
there's one goose, he's been in my way for over
five years now, he, she, of the mutated head and
wattle supreme, she points her beak at the sky
and screams insanely, she doesn't know how to budge,
she is my brother."

"I know that goose," Peter said,
"she may be more than your brother. She bit me twice
once, she's guarding your tree, she's only
ten yards away, she eats and shits, sometimes
she swims with her rubber feet, it's always a joy
seeing her—but staying away—she, he, is
'exempt from the hole' and she eats flowers too
although she's not a squirrel and doesn't have fingers."

"And that was lying awake in a room, wasn't it,"
I said, "and feeling looked at by the room,"
I'm quoting you, "and there was another room
watching from far off yet still inside the
room"—I'm quoting—"you are a fugit too
and you write love letters."

                    "I always look at the end
of a poem," he said, "and what I did I like
though I can't paraphrase it, you'd get it wrong
the same as me if you tried, in fact I'm shocked
more than a little at my violins and
once or twice even bells and once a gong oh;
I'm sorry about that gong but it had something

to do with inside and outside and the hole
'lifting,' a weird concept I know, and as I
said, 'there is no culprit.' "

                                      "I measured the tree
and it was thirty-four hands," I said, "but it wasn't
just the size, it seems it was carried from someplace
else and the top branches were as if a
separate world that one brain just couldn't manage
and the life was different above than it was below,
it was so huge, and there was a storm today
Sept. 9, 2004, and the water
roared on its way south, and two umbrellas
met in front of me and hardly noticed
each other they were so busy fighting the wind,
and God knows what the largemouth bass were doing
and the stocked trout and the vicious turtles, their beaks
clanging, water rushing out the nose holes,
and there were ducks shivering in the flooded
rose o' Sharons, their necks pulled in, oh yeah!"

p. 63: Alicia Ostriker's essay "Ecclesiastes as Witness" appears in her book *For the Love of God: The Bible as an Open Book* (New Brunswick, N.J.: Rutgers University Press, 2007).

p. 79: Here are three versions of the "sentence that governed / everything" from Ecclesiastes 3:11:

The New English Bible: "He has made everything to suit its time; moreover he has given men a sense of time past and future, but no comprehension of God's work from beginning to end."

King James: ". . . he hath set the world in their heart, so that no man can find out the work that God maketh from the beginning to the end."

The Tanakh (the Jewish Bible): "He also puts eternity in their mind, but without man ever guessing, from first to last, all the things that God brings to pass."

p. 81: "Sir Arthur" refers to the poet Arthur Vogelsang.

p. 82: Jeremiah Ostriker, Alicia Ostriker's husband, is a world-renowned physicist and astronomer.

Credits

"The Preacher," which first appeared in *American Poetry Review*, was published in a chapbook by Sarabande in 2007.

"Rose in Your Teeth" appeared in *Along These Rivers: Poetry and Photography from Pittsburgh*, edited by Judith Robinson and published by Quadrant Publishing.

"What For?" won a Pushcart Prize for 2008.

Poems in this volume have appeared in the following journals:

Alaska Review: "Save the Last Dance for Me"

The Cortland Review: "Glut"

Five Points: "Bronze Roosters," "What For?," "Flute II," "Stomachs," "Jew," "My Dear," "Death by Wind," "Rose in Your Teeth"

Kestrel: "What Then?"

Natural Bridges: "Traveling Backwards," "Dream III"

The New Yorker: "Asphodel," "Love Box," "Lorca"

Nextbook: "Spaghetti," "Rukeyser"

The Poetry Paper: "Diogenes," "My Dear," "Flute"

Teseret: "From Where I Sit," "59 N. Sitgreaves"

TriQuarterly: "Thom McCann," "Blue Like That"